Hippopotamuses

by Kari Schuetz

BELLWETHER MEDIA · MINNEAPOLIS, MN

Note to Librarians, Teachers, and Parents:

Blastoff! Readers are carefully developed by literacy experts and combine standards-based content with developmentally appropriate text.

Level 1 provides the most support through repetition of high-frequency words, light text, predictable sentence patterns, and strong visual support.

Level 2 offers early readers a bit more challenge through varied simple sentences, increased text load, and less repetition of high-frequency words.

Level 3 advances early-fluent readers toward fluency through increased text and concept load, less reliance on visuals, longer sentences, and more literary language.

Level 4 builds reading stamina by providing more text per page, increased use of punctuation, greater variation in sentence patterns, and increasingly challenging vocabulary.

Level 5 encourages children to move from "learning to read" to "reading to learn" by providing even more text, varied writing styles, and less familiar topics.

Whichever book is right for your reader, Blastoff! Readers are the perfect books to build confidence and encourage a love of reading that will last a lifetime!

This edition first published in 2012 by Bellwether Media, Inc.

No part of this publication may be reproduced in whole or in part without written permission of the publisher. For information regarding permission, write to Bellwether Media, Inc., Attention: Permissions Department, 5357 Penn Avenue South, Minneapolis, MN 55419.

Library of Congress Cataloging-in-Publication Data
Schuetz, Kari.
  Hippopotamuses / by Kari Schuetz.
     p. cm. – (Blastoff! Readers: Animal Safari)
Includes bibliographical references and index.
  Summary: "Developed by literacy experts for students in kindergarten through grade three, this book introduces hippopotamuses to young readers through leveled text and related photos"–Provided by publisher.
  ISBN 978-1-60014-606-0 (hardcover : alk. paper)
  1. Hippopotamidae–Juvenile literature. I. Title.
  QL737.U57S38 2011
  599.63'5–dc22   2011008189

Printed in the United States of America, North Mankato, MN.
080111   1187

Contents

What Are Hippopotamuses?

Hippopotamuses are huge animals. They are also called hippos.

Hippos in Water

Hippos live in
lakes and rivers.
Water keeps their
bodies cool.

A reddish **liquid** protects their skin from the hot sun.

Hippos are too heavy to float. **Webbed feet** help them move in water.

Grazing

Hippos come
out of the water
late in the day.
They **graze**
on grasses.

Pods

Hippos live in groups called **pods**. Most pods have 10 to 30 hippos.

A male hippo
leads a pod.
It fights other
males for females
and **territory**.

Fighting

Hippos open their mouths wide when they fight. They show their large teeth.

Then hippos swing their heads and **bellow** loudly. Charge!

Glossary

bellow—to make a deep roar

graze—to feed on grasses

liquid—something that flows like water

pods—groups of hippopotamuses that live together

territory—the area where an animal or group of animals lives

webbed feet—feet with thin skin connecting the toes

To Learn More

AT THE LIBRARY

Barbé-Julien, Colette. *Little Hippopotamuses.* Milwaukee, Wisc.: Gareth Stevens Pub., 2006.

Murray, Marjorie Dennis. *Hippo Goes Bananas!* New York, N.Y.: Marshall Cavendish, 2006.

Pingry, Patricia A. *Baby Hippopotamus.* Nashville, Tenn.: CandyCane Press, 2004.

ON THE WEB

Learning more about hippopotamuses is as easy as 1, 2, 3.

1. Go to www.factsurfer.com.

2. Enter "hippopotamuses" into the search box.

3. Click the "Surf" button and you will see a list of related Web sites.

With factsurfer.com, finding more information is just a click away.

Index

The images in this book are reproduced through the courtesy of: Eric Isselée, front cover; Tony Heald / naturepl.com, p. 5; Christian Heinrich / Photolibrary, p. 7; Henry Wilson, pp. 9, 21; Peter Scoones / naturepl.com, p. 11; Robert Harding Images / Masterfile, p. 13; Juan Martinez, p. 15; Graeme Shannon, p. 17; Johan Swanepoel, p. 19.